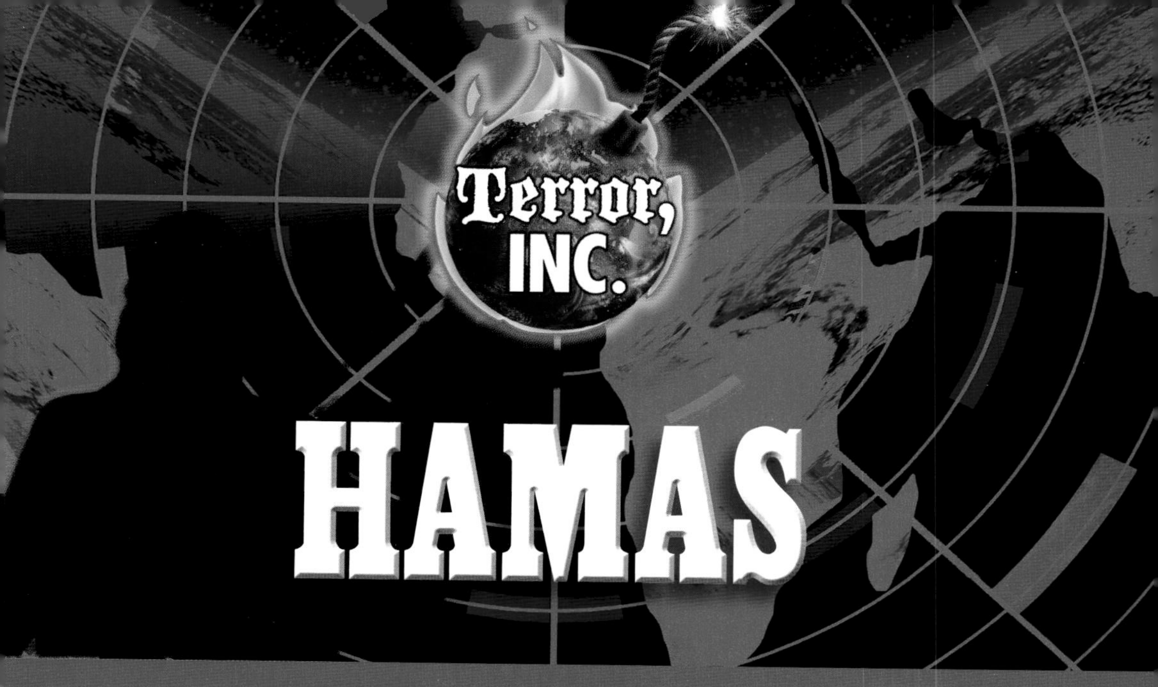

Terror, INC.

HAMAS

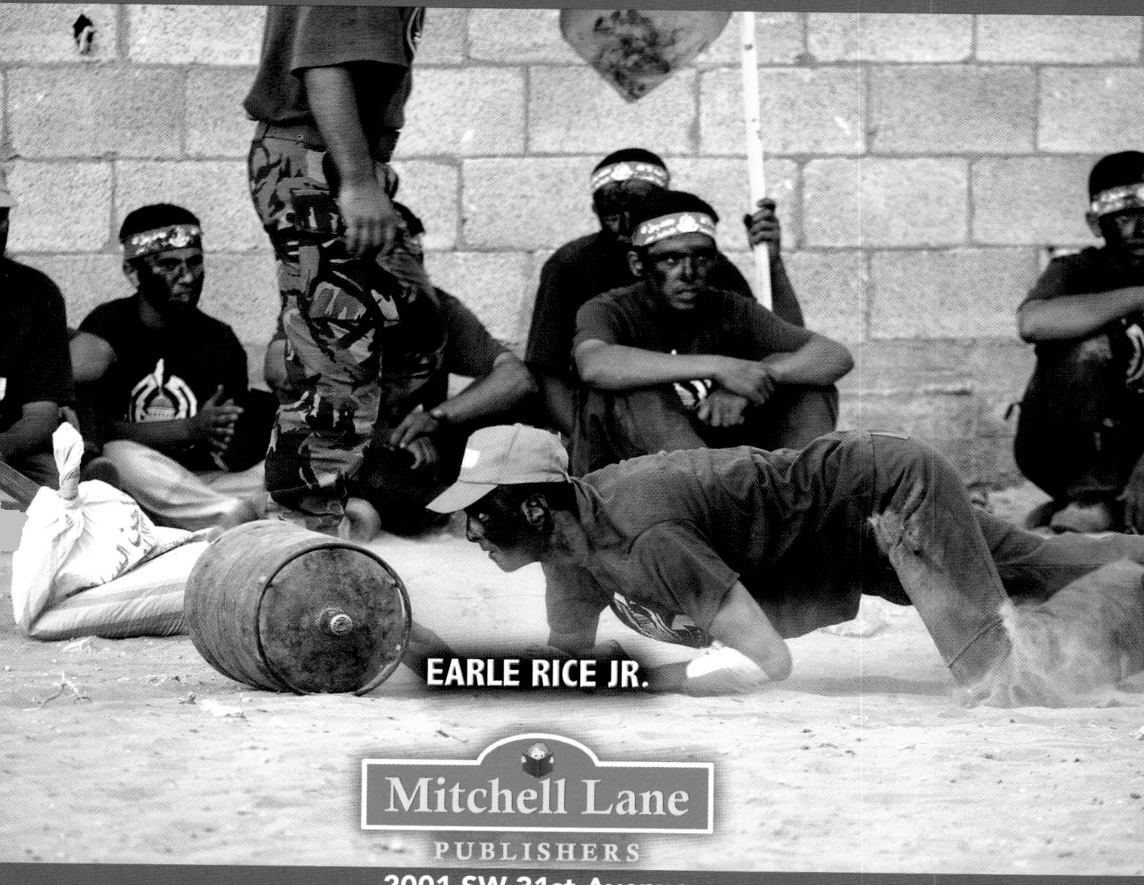

EARLE RICE JR.

Mitchell Lane
PUBLISHERS
2001 SW 31st Avenue
Hallandale, FL 33009
www.mitchelllane.com

Printing 1 2 3 4 5 6 7 8

ABOUT THE COVER: Hamas fighters look on while a fellow militant undergoes training in Gaza City in the Gaza Strip under the direction of a drillmaster. These Palestinian fighters will later use the military skills they learn here to attack Israeli settlements and try to force Israeli settlers to leave the occupied territories. Hamas, a militant organization formed in 1987, aims to establish a Palestinian state and abolish Israel.

ABOUT THE AUTHOR: Earle Rice Jr. is a former senior design engineer and technical writer in the aerospace, electronic-defense, and nuclear industries. He has devoted full time to his writing since 1993, specializing in military and counterinsurgency subjects. Earle is the author of more than 80 published books. He is listed in *Who's Who in America* and is a member of the Society of Children's Book Writers and Illustrators, the League of World War I Aviation Historians, the Air Force Association, and the Disabled American Veterans.

Library of Congress Cataloging-in-Publication Data
Names: Rice, Earle, author.
Title: Hamas / by Earle Rice Jr.
Description: Hallandale, FL : Mitchell Lane Publishers, [2018] | Series: Terror inc | Includes bibliographical references and index.
Identifiers: LCCN 2017009123 | ISBN 9781680200515 (library bound)
Subjects: LCSH: Harakat al-Muqāwamah al-'Islāmiyyah—History.
Classification: LCC JQ1830.A98 R53 2018 | DDC 324.25695/3083—dc23
LC record available at https://lccn.loc.gov/2017009123

eBook ISBN: 978-1-68020-052-2

Contents

Words in **bold** throughout can be found in the Glossary.

Foreword

Terror has plagued the world since men in caves flailed away at each other with sticks and stones. As the world emerged from **primeval** times and entered the ancient age, humans clashed on a larger, more advanced scale called warfare. Slings, arrows, and spears wrought havoc in the Golden Age of Greece and stained the glory that was Rome. Ethnic and religious strife followed close behind. In medieval times, crusading Christians and faith-based Muslims carved a bloody path across the Middle East with sword, lance, and scimitar in the causes of God and Allah. Americans engaged in "total war" for the first time during the Civil War, a war pitting brother against brother and fathers against sons at a cost of 750,000 lives. The 20th century introduced global wars that claimed the lives of tens of millions of combatants and civilians.

Today, international terrorism has become a form of warfare. The U.S. Department of Defense defines terrorism as "the unlawful use of—or threatened use of—force or violence against individuals or property to **coerce** or intimidate governments or societies, often to achieve political, religious, or ideological objectives." In many parts of the world, terror is a way of life. Militant Muslim extremists seek to rid Muslim countries of what they view as the **profane** influence of the West and replace their governments with fundamentalist regimes based on their interpretation of the religion of **Islam**.

The American way of life changed forever when 19 Islamist terrorists flew fuel-laden aircraft—flying bombs—into the World Trade Center in New York City and the Pentagon in Washington, DC, on September 11, 2001. Today, radical Islamist groups continue to be America's main threat of terrorism.

It should be noted that only a small minority of Muslims believe in terror as a strategy. A recent Gallup poll indicated that just seven percent of the world's 1.6 billion Muslims support extremist views of terrorism. The purpose of this book is to alert and enlighten the reader about that seven percent, while affirming the essential righteousness of the other 93 percent of Islam's followers. Peace be upon the gentle of mind, spirit, and deed.

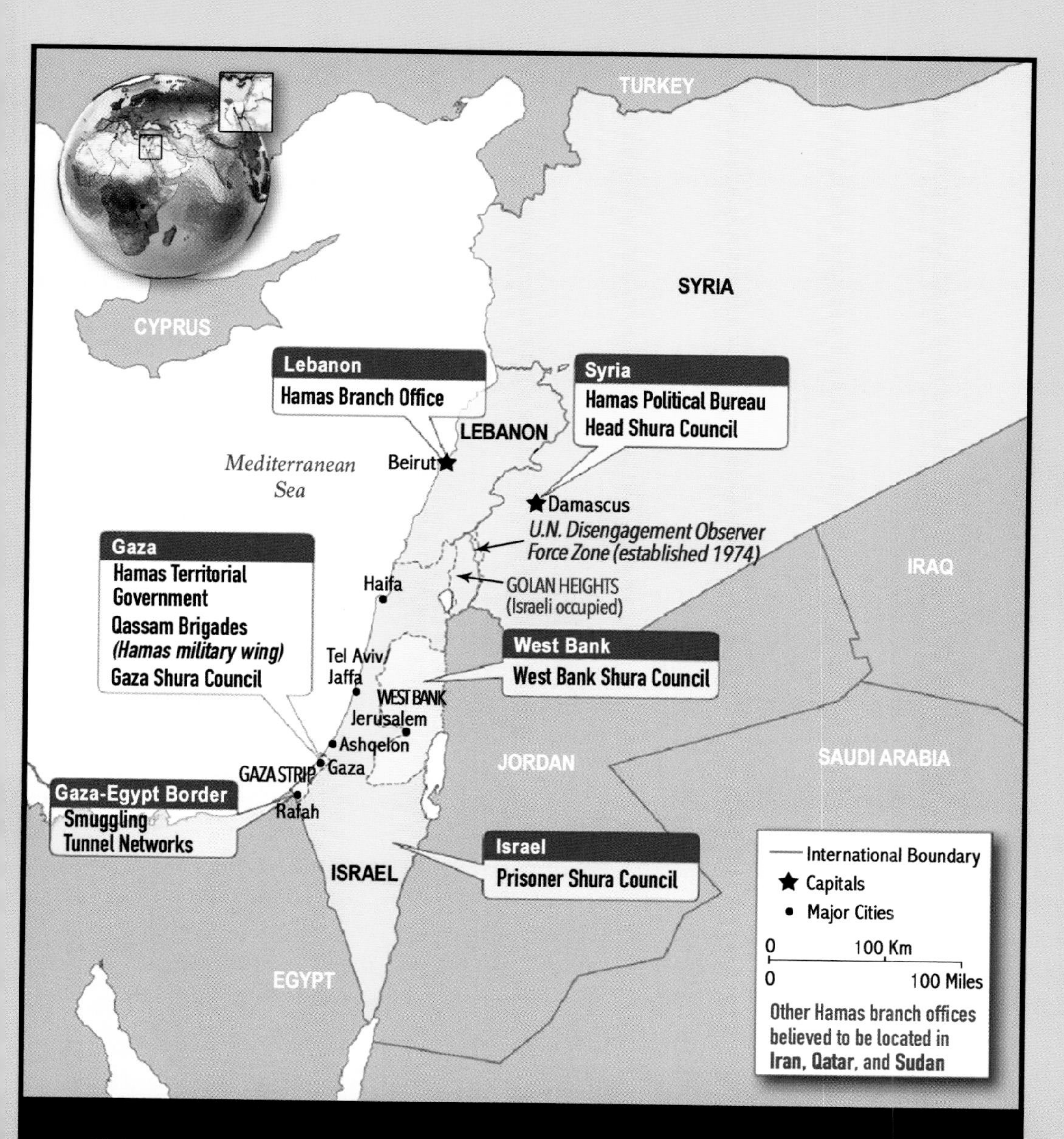

This map illustrates the wide influence that Hamas exhibits as a major player in the ongoing Arab-Israeli conflict. Founded just 30 years ago, Hamas has become increasingly important in the region's politics.

Palestinian suicide bomber Abdel Basset Odeh brandishes an M16 rifle in one hand and a fake Israeli identity card in the other in this photo supplied by his family. Odeh, a member of the militant group Izz ad-Deen al-Qassam Brigade, disguised himself as a woman, hid an explosive belt beneath his feminine clothing, and blew himself up in the lobby of the Park Hotel in the coastal city of Netanya, Israel. Palestinians hailed him as a hero and a martyr for an act that claimed the lives of 30 innocent people and wounded many more.

CHAPTER 1
Bitter Root

"Explosions aren't that strange in Netanya," observed Itzik Doublis in a 2012 interview with Ben Hartman of *The Jerusalem Post*. Doublis was a longtime resident of the Israeli coastal city. He was hinting about Netanya's reputation for organized crime. "When the ambulances and the police kept coming we knew something was wrong, that this wasn't criminal." Doublis was referring to the Park Hotel bombing on March 27, 2002, an event that had shattered his community ten years earlier. He added that the city's sense of security never fully recovered, but "your brain manages to forget, there's always other things in this country you can focus on."[1]

A decade after the explosion that rocked Netanya, Hartman came to the city to interview survivors of the bombing. "I'll never forget it was raining and drizzling outside and when I got there all the windows were blown out," recalled first responder Marc Kahlberg, who had commanded the tourism branch of the Netanya police in 2002. "We went in and just pulled out whatever we could, put bodies and body parts on tables, it was horrible."[2] The unspeakable horrors still linger in the minds of all Netanyans.

Joel Leyden remembers what often seems like yesterday to all those who witnessed its pain and destruction. Leyden, a journalist with the Israel News Agency, was visiting his in-laws in Netanya with his wife and newborn daughter to share Passover dinner. He recalled that their arrival was met with "cloudless skies, sun drenched streets, [and] birds chirping as the spring weather smiled."[3]

Later, in the carpeted living room of his in-laws, the Leydens heard a clap of thunder. A light drizzle began to fall. Then they heard an ambulance siren. Moments later, a second and a third siren screamed past their building. Alarmed, they turned on the television and received the first reports of what would later be called the Passover Massacre. Leyden wrote:

> In one of the most brutal terrorist attacks sustained by Israel, an Islamic suicide terror bomber from the **Hamas** terrorist organization walked into Netanya's Park Hotel on March 27, 2002. He strode pass the reception desk and calmly walked into the main dining hall. As elderly Jews and children were sitting over matza and chicken soup, the terrorist detonated a lethal charge, murdering 29 [later 30], and wounding 140. The dead included babies, grandmothers, and six married couples.[4]

Joel Leyden reacted to the news as most journalists would. Ignoring the wishes of his family to stay and observe the Passover meal with them, he rushed to the scene of the devastating blast two blocks away to report the story.

Outside the hotel lay dismembered and blood-soaked bodies covered with blue blankets. Shards of shattered glass from blown-out windows in the lobby and on the second floor littered the ground. Leyden proceeded into the lobby to find it darkened from loss of power and pooled with water from the sprinkler system's broken pipes. People young and old passed him as they staggered out of the hotel, silent, dazed, and frozen in shock. Where moments earlier there had been gaiety, laughter, and life, there was now an eerie, death-filled quiet.

More than 250 people had gathered at the hotel to observe the Passover Seder, the ritual feast that marks the beginning of Passover (the deliverance of the Jewish people from slavery in

Egypt). Blast victims included children and some Holocaust survivors; many were senior citizens over seventy.

Leyden spoke briefly with Netanya's mayor, Miriam Feyerberg. She said that Israelis must stay strong and continue with their lives as usual, otherwise the terrorists would win. She added, "In recent days, these terrorist groups have begun describing their actions as acts of 'resistance,' but resistance is not blowing up children and babies."[5]

The suicide bomber was Abdel Basset Odeh, a 25-year-old Palestinian resident of the nearby West Bank town of Tulkarm. He belonged to the radical Palestinian terrorist group known as

Israeli first responders remove a victim of a suicide bomber's blast in the lobby of the Park Hotel in Netanya, Israel, on March 27, 2002. More than 250 Israelis were observing the Passover Seder at the hotel at the time of the explosion.

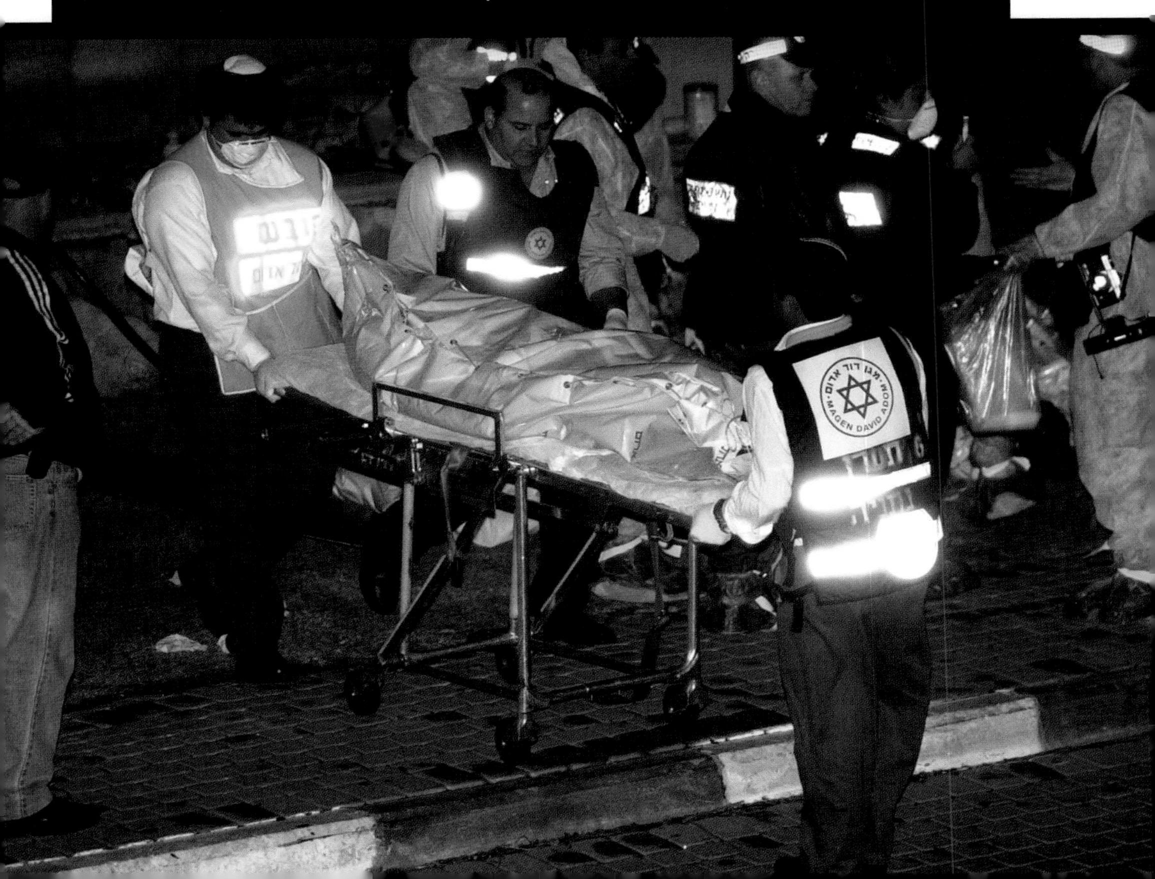

The bombed-out interior of the Park Hotel, in Netanya, Israel, bears witness to the horrendous devastation wrought by a Palestinian suicide bomber. Emergency workers search through the wreckage for signs of undiscovered victims.

Hamas (hah-MAHSS). Palestinians hailed him as a hero, turned him into a poster boy for their movement, and even held a soccer tournament to honor him.

Arabs have lived in Palestine for centuries. As part of what is known as the Holy Land, Palestine is sacred to Christians, Jews, and Muslims alike. Palestinians have never had a nation-state to call their own. For their entire existence, they have been ruled by someone else, most recently by the Israelis. Therein lies the source of their anger and the object of their resistance.

Starting in 1516, Palestine became part of the Ottoman Empire, which sprawled across the Middle East, North Africa, and parts of Europe. Its capital was in Constantinople (today known as Istanbul), Turkey. The late nineteenth century saw the early stirrings of the modern-day state of Israel. In his book *Der Judenstaat* (The Jewish State), published in 1896, a Hungarian Jew named Theodor Herzl visualized a permanent Jewish homeland. The following year he founded the **Zionist** Organization in Basel, Switzerland. Its primary goal was establishing that homeland in Palestine.

At the start of World War I in 1914, Turkey allied with Germany. In 1916, Britain and France made a secret treaty called the Sykes-Picot Agreement. It would divide up the crumbling Ottoman Empire almost equally between themselves when the war was over. Mesopotamia (southern Iraq), Transjordan (Jordan), and part of the Arabian Peninsula would go to Britain. France would take Lebanon, Syria, northern Iraq, and southeastern Anatolia (the Asia Minor part of Turkey). Because of its importance to three religions, Palestine would be under international control.

On November 2, 1917, the British government issued the Balfour Declaration to the Zionists, which stated

> His Majesty's Government view with favour the establishment in Palestine of a national home for the Jewish people, and will use their best endeavours to facilitate the achievement of this object, it being clearly understood that nothing shall be done which may prejudice the civil and religious rights of existing non-Jewish communities in Palestine, or the rights and political status enjoyed by Jews in any other country.[6]

In 1920, the victorious Allies divided up the Ottoman Empire according to the Sykes-Picot Agreement at a conference in San Remo, Italy. Britain was awarded the **mandate** for Palestine, rather than putting it under international control. Under the terms of the mandate, the British began laying the foundation for the establishment of a Jewish state according to the Balfour Declaration. That set down the root of the Palestinian-Israeli conflict. From the Palestinian perspective, the root is deep and bitter.

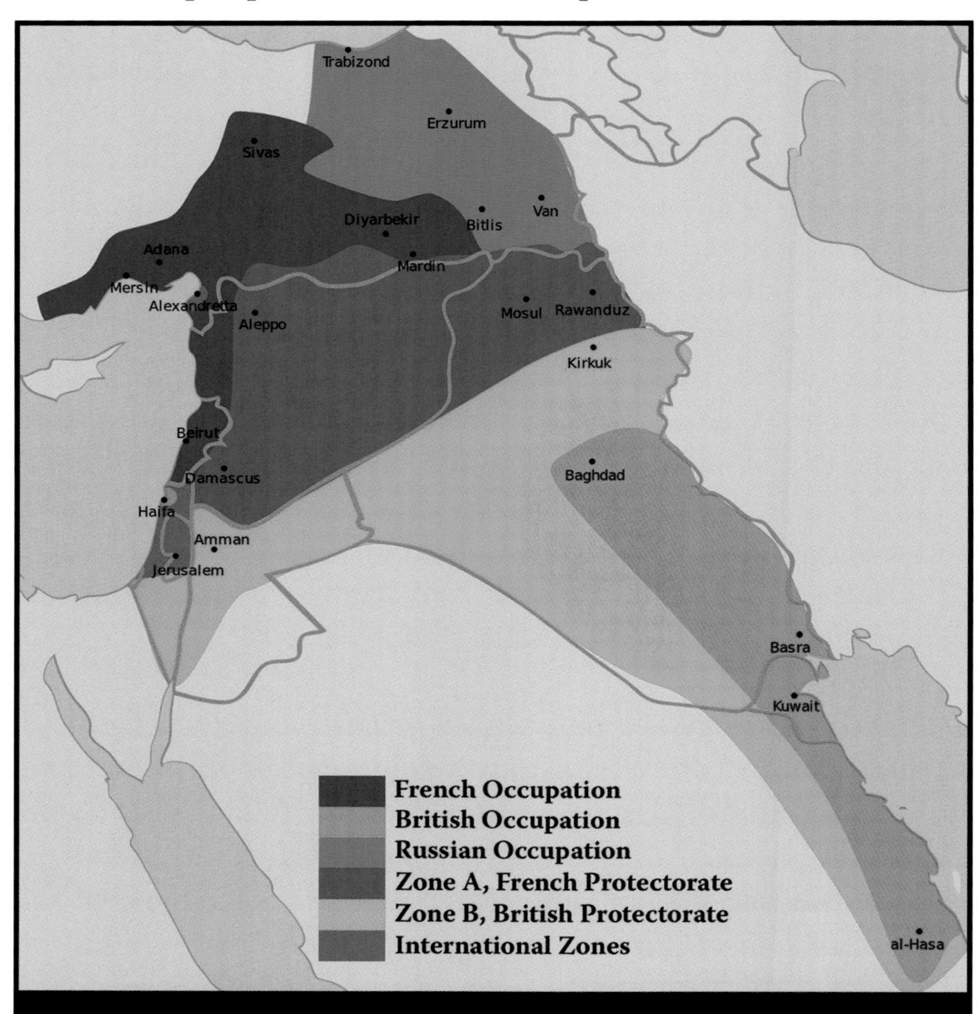

A secret convention held between Great Britain and France—with the assent of Imperial Russia—in May 1916, led to what became known as the Sykes-Picot Agreement. The agreement laid out the terms for dissolving the Ottoman Empire, which divided Turkish-held Syria, Iraq, Lebanon, and Palestine into various British- and French-administered areas. Russia was allotted Constantinople (Istanbul) and control of the Dardanelles, though that didn't happen.

Passover Plot

In the afternoon hours of March 27, 2002, Abdel Basset Odeh methodically prepared himself for the most important task of his 25-year existence. He stood before a mirror in his quarters in Tulkarm, a city in the West Bank of Palestine. He shaved off his beard and mustache. Now smooth-faced, he carefully applied makeup and donned a woman's straight-hair wig. Pleased with his new appearance, he slipped into a pair of feminine-cut blue jeans, a brown shirt, a brown leather jacket with a leopard-print collar, and a pair of women's shoes. He tucked a fake Israeli ID card with a woman's name in his jacket pocket to complete his transformation.

Abdel Basset Odeh

Abbas al-Sayyid, head of the military wing of Hamas in Tulkarm, strapped an explosive belt on Odeh and explained how to detonate it. A camera filmed Odeh reading his will aloud, while wearing a Hamas head-band and holding an M16 rifle.

At the appointed hour, Fathi Khatib, another Hamas member, arrived to pick up Odeh in a newly purchased car with a yellow Israeli license plate. Khatib drove Odeh to Netanya—a distance of just under 50 miles—and dropped him off near the Park Hotel. Odeh walked confidently and undeterred through the hotel lobby and into the large dining hall where guests were celebrating Passover.

At 7:20 P.M., he blew himself up.

Hassan al-Banna, an Egyptian schoolteacher, founded the Muslim Brotherhood (MB) in Ismailia, Egypt, in 1928. It became the largest and strongest religious, political, and social movement in Egypt and later spread to other Muslim countries. Egypt's military government legalized the Brotherhood in April 2011. Today, many Arabs in other nations support it and countless Muslims around the world admire it.

CHAPTER 2
Partition and Protest

In 1921, Syrian-born Sheikh Izz ad-Din al-Qassam arrived in Haifa, a coastal city in Palestine, and began work as a Muslim preacher. His name meant "Might of the Faith." Bearded and white-robed, he called for a revival of Islamic values and a rejection of Western ways through jihad ("holy war"). His radical creed combined faith and firearms. It would serve as a model for future generations of Islamists.

Qassam exhorted his fellow Arabs to rise up against their "**infidel**" British overlords. He denounced their plan to create a Jewish homeland in Palestine. And he railed against the successive waves of Jewish immigrants who had begun flooding the Holy Land. In 1922, the **League of Nations** limited the boundary of Palestine to the area west of the Jordan River. It made the area east of the river, called Transjordan (now Jordan), a separate mandate. The two mandates took effect in 1923. Because the mandates were unclear, however, various parties interpreted them differently. Zionists felt that Britain wasn't promoting a Jewish homeland vigorously enough and was unduly restricting Jewish immigration. Palestinians still opposed the idea of a Jewish national home. They feared that the British were delivering Palestine to the Zionists by allowing too many Jews to immigrate. Arab fears and resentment gave rise to a Palestinian national movement.

In 1928, Hassan al-Banna, an Egyptian schoolteacher, founded the Muslim Brotherhood (MB) in Ismailia, Egypt. "The Muslim Brotherhood is a movement loathed and feared in many parts of the world," writes Islamic scholar Azzam Tamimi, "but loved and supported by millions of Arabs and admired by many more millions of Muslims around the world."[1] Its social services institutions provided an ideal tool for Islamists to radicalize and recruit Muslim youth. The MB, more than any other Islamist organization, would profoundly influence Hamas in the latter half of the century.

Arabs rioted in Hebron in 1929 to protest British policies and Zionist activities. The following year, Qassam moved from preaching and circulating ideas to **overt** political activism that would soon lead him to violence. He founded the Black Hand (*Al-Kaff al-Aswad*), an anti-Zionist and anti-British organization that began attacking Jewish targets in northern Palestine. In the early 1930s, an influx into Palestine of Jewish refugees from Nazi Germany and Poland further angered Arabs.

British police killed Qassam in a shootout near Jenin in 1935. Ironically, his grave now lies in Israel, the Jewish homeland whose creation he fought in vain to prevent. An inscription on his headstone reads, in part: "He is our Sheikh, al-Qassam, the first to raise the flag of jihad with us to support the faith."[2]

The Black Hand achieved only limited success during its brief existence, but it inspired future terrorist groups. Some of its surviving members took part in the Great Arab Revolt of 1936–39 in Palestine. The revolt, partially inspired by the shooting of Qassam, sought Palestinian independence and a halt to Jewish immigration. Though it failed to achieve its goals, it gave birth to a national identity.

The British suppressed the revolt. They also put tight limits on the number of Jews who could come to Palestine. When World War II ended in 1945, tens of thousands of Holocaust survivors tried to enter Palestine. The British refused to admit them. Tensions among Jews, Arabs, and the British intensified. The British decided to withdraw. In November, 1947, the United Nations agreed to partition Palestine into separate Jewish and

Arab states. Fighting broke out between the two sides. On May 14, 1948, the Jews proclaimed the independent state of Israel, and the British withdrew from Palestine. Five neighboring Arab states immediately attacked Israel, touching off the Arab-Israeli War of 1948. When it ended the following year, Israel held territories beyond those set by the U.N. plan. In addition, Egypt occupied the Gaza Strip, while Jordan took over the West Bank. About 700,000 Palestinians fled to neighboring Arab nations.

Full-scale Arab-Israeli wars broke out again in 1956 (Suez Canal Crisis), 1967 (Six-Day War), and 1973 (Yom Kippur War). After the Six-Day War, Israel occupied the Gaza Strip, the West Bank, Egypt's Sinai Peninsula, and Syria's Golan Heights. The war brought about a million Palestinians under Israeli control.

Israeli soldiers guard Arab prisoners in a barbed-wire enclosure in Jerusalem on August 31, 1967, during the Arab-Israeli Six-Day War.

Palestinians played a large part in the Arab-Israeli struggle. The Palestine Liberation Organization (PLO), which had been founded in 1964 under Yasser Arafat, emerged from the conflicts as the representative of the Palestinian people.

In 1978, Egypt and Israel signed the Camp David Accords, an agreement designed to settle their disputes. It also called for a five-year transitional period leading to self-governance for the residents of the Gaza Strip and the West Bank. Supposedly, the future of those territories would be determined later. No such arrangements were made following the agreement.

In 1982, Israel invaded Lebanon and drove the PLO out of southern Lebanon, where it had launched a number of attacks, and later out of northern Lebanon. Arafat relocated PLO headquarters to Tunisia. The loss of a military option in Lebanon dealt a blow to its national movement. After Israel's withdrawal from most of Lebanon in 1985, some PLO members trickled back into southern Lebanon.

In 1983, Shiekh Ahmad Yassin, a paraplegic teacher of religion and the Arabic language, told his followers to begin secretly gathering firearms. Yassin had arrived in the refugee neighborhood of Al-Sabra in Gaza City when he was a boy. He became a leading figure in the Islamic revitalization project in the Gaza Strip. The project was fostered by the Muslim Brotherhood, which had opened its first branch in Palestine in Jerusalem in 1946.

When Israeli authorities found weapons in his home two years later, Yassin said they were for defense against rival Palestinian groups. In 1986, Yassin authorized the creation of a security apparatus to enforce Islamic social norms.

In 1987, waves of protesting Palestinians swept through the Gaza Strip and the West Bank. The First Intifada ("uprising" in Arabic) had begun. Yassin declared: "The intifada will go on and the suffering of the Palestinian people will continue. But so will our absolute determination to pursue the struggle."[3]

Palestine Liberation Organization

The Palestine Liberation Organization (PLO) is a political body that represents the Palestinian people. The PLO was conceived at the first Arab League summit meeting in Cairo in January 1964. It was founded four months later at a Palestinian Congress in East Jerusalem. Its charter defined it as a **secular** organization formed for the purpose of reclaiming the Palestinian homeland from the Jewish Zionists through popular armed struggle (jihad): "[I]t is a national duty to repulse the Zionist, imperial invasion . . . and to purge the Zionist presence from Palestine."[4]

The Palestinian Congress appointed Ahmad al-Shuqayri, an official of the Arab League, to head the new organization as chairman of the PLO Executive Committee. After the Six-Day War of 1967, the victorious Israelis seized all unoccupied Palestine territory. **Fatah** ("conquest" in Arabic), the PLO's leading guerrilla group, took over control of the organization. Yasser Arafat assumed the role of chairman. He remained chairman until his death in 2004. Mahmoud Abbas replaced him.

Both the United States and Israel considered the PLO a terrorist organization until the Madrid Conference of 1991, which led to a peace treaty in 1994. The PLO remains the recognized representative of the Palestinian people, though it has surrendered much of its influence to the Palestinian Authority, the governing body of the West Bank and Gaza.

In this handout photo from the PLO, Palestinian leader Yasser Arafat (left) and Palestinian Prime Minister Mahmoud Abbas attend an executive committee meeting in Arafat's office August 3, 2003 in the West Bank city of Ramallah.

Two Israeli border police officers thread their way through the debris from a bomb blast in downtown Jerusalem on March 3, 1996. Behind them, bomb squad members and firefighters comb the wreckage of a bus targeted by a Hamas suicide bomber, the second terrorist bombing in a week. The blast killed 19 people and injured dozens more.

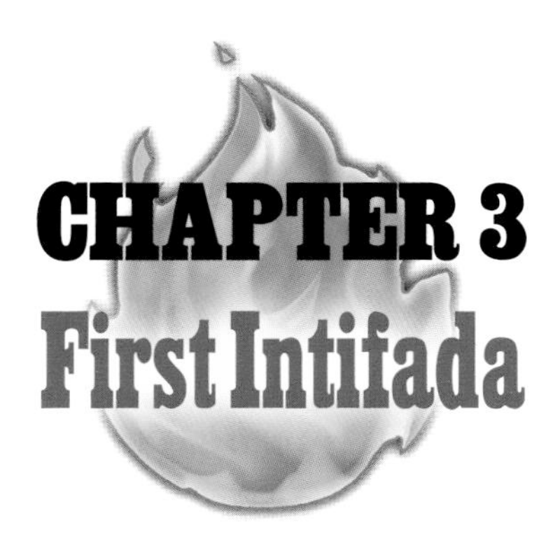

CHAPTER 3
First Intifada

On December 9, 1987, in the rain and gloom of a winter's day, a truck driven by a member of the Israeli Defense Forces (IDF) struck a car of Arab workers in the Jabalia refugee camp in the Gaza Strip. The collision killed four Palestinians. Rumors that the collision was intentional circulated quickly and touched off what came to be known as the First Intifada. Violence, championed by the Palestinian **Islamic Jihad**, quickly spread to the West Bank and led to the birth of Hamas.

Hamas—meaning "zeal" in Arabic—is an **acronym** for *harakat al-muqawama al-islamiya*, or Islamic Resistance Movement. Founded by Yassin and six members of his inner circle, it emerged from the Muslim Brotherhood. It provided the MB with a means for joining the Palestinian struggle against Israel.

Hamas published its charter in August 1988. It reads in part, "The Islamic Resistance Movement believes that the land of Palestine is an Islamic ***Waqf*** endowment consecrated for future Moslem [Muslim] generations until Judgment Day. It, or any part of it, should not be squandered; or any part of it, should not be given up." The charter adds, "there is no solution to the Palestine question except through jihad."[1] It further calls for the destruction of Israel and the establishment of an Islamic society in Palestine.

Hamas carried out its first attack against Israel in 1989. It abducted and killed two Israeli soldiers. Hamas planned to use their bodies to bargain for the release of Israeli-held Hamas prisoners. The IDF responded by arresting Yassin and sentencing him to two life terms in prison.

In 1991, Hamas formed a new armed wing, the Izz ad-Din al-Qassam Brigades. Sheikh Salah Shehadeh, an Egyptian-educated former Muslim Brotherhood activist, headed it. The name honored the Islamist activist who fought against the British and Jewish settlers in Palestine in the 1930s.

While Hamas prepared to escalate violence against Israel, U.S. President George H. W. Bush and Soviet President Mikhail Gorbachev convened the Madrid Conference in October 1991. "The time has come to put an end to the Arab-Israeli conflict,"[2] President Bush declared. Despite its honorable intentions, the conference closed with little more than an agreement for the parties to keep talking.

After an Israeli police officer was kidnapped and murdered in 1992, Israeli Prime Minister Yitzhak Rabin ordered the deportation of more than 400 Hamas and Islamic Jihad activists to then-Israeli-occupied Lebanon. While in exile, the activists built a relationship with **Hezbollah,** a militant Islamist group based in Lebanon. They also cultivated cordial relations with Fatah, one of the largest Islamist activist groups within the PLO.

On September 13, 1993, Israel and the PLO signed the Oslo Accords in Norway. The secretly negotiated agreement outlined an agenda for peace and final status negotiations. It provided interim Palestinian **autonomy** in the Gaza Strip and West Bank. It also helped to bring the First Intifada to a close. The Accords posed a serious blow to Hamas. The group must now confront both Israel and the future Palestinian Authority (PA), which would be created in 1994. At the same time, it must continue its armed struggle against Israel. Most critically, it must do so without alienating popular opinion that favored an end to hostilities and a return to Palestinian homelands. Hamas rejected the Accords outright and stepped up its attacks against Israel.

By late 1993, Hamas's terror operations had become increasingly aimed at Israeli civilians. They shifted now to suicide tactics.

This change in tactics reflected their recent associations with Hezbollah, which had popularized the technique. Over the next five years, Hamas suicide bombers relentlessly attacked civilian targets in Israel. One of the first and most notable occurred in the Israeli town of Afula on April 6, 1994. A 19-year-old Palestinian suicide bomber killed eight Israelis and wounded 34 more.

"I support martyrdom operations in Israel," said Hamas activist Gazan Mohammed Yasji. "Let them know how it feels to see civilians die. Suicide bombs make me feel stronger because I penetrate their security."[3]

In February–March 1996, Yasser Arafat—now back in Gaza after three decades of exile—cracked down on Hamas after a series of suicide bombings. Following hawkish Benjamin Netanyahu's election as Israeli prime minister in May 1996, however, Arafat was forced to cultivate Hamas's support to put pressure on Israeli decision-makers.

On September 25, 1997, **Mossad** agents failed in an attempt to assassinate Khaled Meshaal, head of Hamas's Political Bureau in Amman, Jordan. Jordanian authorities captured the agents, and Israel released Sheikh Yassin to secure their return. After an absence of eight years, Yassin reestablished his position as spiritual leader of Hamas. He shifted its focus back to the Palestinian territories. His release strengthened the local leadership of Hamas and deepened a growing tension between the local and foreign bases of the movement.

Hamas persisted in rejecting the Oslo Accords. It did so without actively rejecting the Palestinian Authority's institutions. At the same time, it did not fully accept them nor the PA's peacemaking policy.

On October 23, 1998, Israel and the Palestinian Authority signed the Wye Memorandum. It intended to clarify mutual responsibilities for implementing Oslo II, the interim agreement

Hooded and bearded, Sheikh Ahmad Yassin, spiritual leader and one of six original founders of Hamas, sits defiantly in front of a rank of his black-faced and camo-garbed followers at a rally.

on the Gaza Strip and West Bank, signed on September 28, 1995. The process broke down several months later.

During the two-week Camp David Summit in July 2000, Israeli Prime Minister Ehud Barak, Palestinian President Yasser Arafat, and U.S. President Bill Clinton failed to reach a peace settlement. Two months later, Israeli opposition leader Ariel Sharon toured the Temple Mount in Jerusalem. The Al-Aqsa Mosque, Islam's third most holy site, forms part of the Temple Mount. Allegedly, the purpose of Sharon's visit was to show that under his government the Temple Mount would remain under Israeli sovereignty. Palestinians saw Sharon's visit as a provocation, however. A riot ensued. Israeli police dispersed stone-throwing demonstrators using tear gas and rubber bullets. Chaos in the streets offered a preview of the Second (or *Al-Aqsa*) Intifada.

Muslim Brotherhood

Supporters of Egyptian President Mohamed Morsi and members of the Muslim Brotherhood chant slogans during a rally on December 14, 2012 in Cairo, Egypt.

The Muslim Brotherhood (MB), or the Society of Muslim Brothers, is a global religious and political movement. It rejects secularism and calls for Muslim nations to establish governments based on Islamic principles and ruled by **Sharia law**. Founded by Sheikh Hassan al-Banna in 1928, the MB is Egypt's oldest and largest Islamist organization.

Banna saw European colonialism in Egypt and the Middle East as a corrupting influence on Muslim society and politics. He hoped to reorganize Egyptian society and develop a modern Egypt based on Islamic ideals. His movement spread throughout North Africa and the Middle East during the 1930s and 1940s.

Today, the Muslim Brotherhood (MB) is widely considered the world's most influential Islamist organization. As such, it has spawned Islamist groups throughout the Arab world, such as al-Qaeda and Hamas. The MB embraces strong anti-Christian and anti-Jewish sentiments. It seeks to revive and spread Islamic principles across the globe.

In recent times, the MB emerged as Egypt's dominant political force. Its candidate, Mohamed Morsi, became Egypt's first democratically elected president in June 2012. After his power-grabbing overreach the following year, the Egyptian military removed him from office. Egyptian defense minister Abdel Fattah el-Sisi replaced him in May 2014.

Female volunteers of the Al Aqsa Martyrs' Brigade stand veiled, with explosives strapped to their midsections. A table in front of them displays a copy of the Quran, a Palestinian flag, and a grenade launcher. The militant group then formed a part of Palestinian leader Yasser Arafat's Fatah movement. During the Second Intifada, the Brigade carried out ten attacks, including four by female suicide bombers. Al Aqsa is the only Palestinian group that accepts and trains women to be martyrs. Unlike Hamas and Islamic Jihad, its ideology features nationalism rather than religious and political Islam.

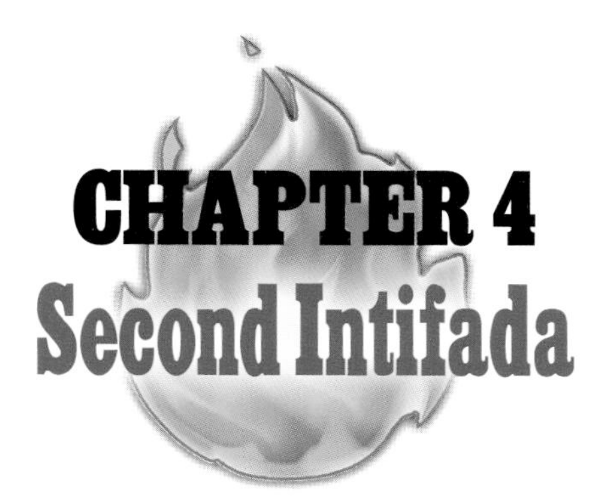

CHAPTER 4
Second Intifada

The Second Intifada opened the door for Hamas and the Palestinian Islamic Jihad to resume violent operations against Israel. Rioting quickly spread to the Gaza Strip. On September 30, 2000, two days into the Intifada, a 12-year-old Palestinian boy was shot dead in a crossfire between Palestinian militants and Israeli soldiers. Less than two weeks later, two Israeli reserve soldiers were mutilated and lynched in retaliation. By year's end, Palestinian deaths numbered 173 against 30 Israeli fatalities. Hopes for a peace settlement declined as casualties rose.

Ariel Sharon's election as Israel's prime minister in February, 2001 did little to calm the troubled waters. Islamic terror attacks served as incentives for Palestinian Authority-linked groups—primarily Fatah—to join the violence lest they lose support among the Palestinian people. The Islamists employed various methods of attack—ambushes, sniper fire, drive-by shootings, car bombings, suicide bombings, and rocket fire.

In 2001, Islamist targets included a Tel Aviv disco, a pizzeria and shopping mall in Jerusalem, and a bus in Haifa. An Amnesty International report on the first full year of fighting condemned the actions of both sides: "Violence has become a part of daily life in Israel and the occupied Territories. . . . More than 570 Palestinians, including 150 children, have been killed by Israeli security forces. More than 150 Israelis, including 30 children, have been killed by Palestinian armed groups and individuals."[1]

Despite the brutal and indiscriminate nature of their attacks, Hamas and Islamic Jihad enjoyed growing popular support for their success in causing heavy Israeli losses with their suicide

bombings. Their rise in public favor was not lost on Fatah. To keep pace with their rival Islamists, Fatah felt obligated to adopt similar lethal tactics.

The year 2002 began with a flurry of activity. On January 3, Israeli commandos seized the 4,000-ton cargo freighter *Karine*, loaded with 50 tons of Iranian-supplied weapons for delivery to the Palestinian Authority. Eleven days later, Israeli operatives in Tulkarm assassinated Raed al-Karmi. He was the leader of the Al Aqsa Martyrs' Brigades, a militant offshoot of Fatah.

In response to the slaying, Fatah recruited Wafa Idris to become the first Palestinian woman suicide bomber. On January 27, she blew herself up in Jerusalem, killing an 81-year-old Israeli man and wounding more than 150 others.

On March 2, another suicide bombing engineered by Al Aqsa Martyrs' Brigades killed 11 people in the Jerusalem neighborhood of Beit Yisrael. The Park Hotel bombing followed less than a month later.

Fatah operative Hussein ash-Sheikh tried to distance Fatah from Hamas. He explained, "The main reason is that Al Aqsa Brigades are nationalist and political, not religious. What the Al Aqsa Brigades did was not a result of hatred of Israel and Jews. . . . The reason was a reaction to Israeli aggression."[2]

The U.S. State Department denied Sheikh's explanation. On March 22, 2002, it declared the Al Aqsa Brigades a "foreign terrorist organization,"[3] alongside Hamas, Islamic Jihad, and al-Qaeda. At the same time, Israel fingered Fatah as the main source of its problems because Hamas was much smaller. Fatah-sponsored operations outweighed those of Hamas and the Islamic Jihad. Israel was forced to mount a large-scale operation to recapture Palestinian refugee camps and eradicate the bases of terrorism.

On March 29, Israel launched Operation Defensive Shield. Israeli forces reoccupied the West Bank and besieged Yasser

Arafat's headquarters in Ramallah. The incursion lasted until May 3. It ended with the recapture of PA-controlled territory. A U.N. casualty report of the period from March 1 to May 7 estimated 497 Palestinian dead and 1,447 wounded, compared to 30 Israeli dead and 127 wounded.

On July 22, Israel struck another major blow at Hamas, dropping a one-ton bomb on a building in Gaza where Hamas's military leader Salah Shehadeh was staying. The blast killed Shehadeh and more than a dozen other people. Within two years, Israel's unrelenting attacks succeeded in assassinating almost the entire upper tier of Hamas leadership. Shaul Mofaz, Israel's former defense minister, later referred to the targeting of Hamas leaders as a plan to "liquidate the terrorists."[4]

The years 2003 and 2004 yielded more of the same in Israel and Palestine. Suicide bombings continued as the favored weapon of Hamas and its fellow Islamists. Hamas co-founder Abdel Aziz Rantissi said, "Since we don't have F16s [fighter jets] or Apache missiles or tanks we have our own weapons to defend ourselves. Believe me, if we had F16s we would never use suicide attacks."[5] So the suicide bombings continued in Haifa, Afula, Jerusalem, and elsewhere in Israel. The Israelis responded with air, missile, and artillery attacks, chiefly across the Gaza Strip.

On March 22, 2004, an Israeli airstrike killed Yassin. Hamas named Abdel Aziz Rantissi as his successor. Less than a month after assuming the leadership of Hamas, another Israeli airstrike assassinated him in Gaza. Hamas leaders went into hiding. The identity of the new leader was kept secret, but was widely believed to be Syrian-based Khaled Meshaal. Israeli operations killed or captured many of Hamas's military leaders in the West Bank, though the group's military and political leadership and civil infrastructure in the Gaza Strip remained almost entirely intact.

What might be called the year's most significant event in the Palestinian-Israeli struggle came with the death of Yasser Arafat

During a symbolic funeral for slain Hamas leader Abdel Aziz Rantissi in the Baghdad suburb of Baladiyat, a young Palestinian boy holds an AK-47 semiautomatic rifle against a photographic backdrop of Hamas leaders. Held on April 18, 2004, the event prompted dozens of families from the Palestinian camp of Haifa to demonstrate in the streets of Baladiyat in protest of Israel's assassination of Rantissi.

in a Paris hospital on November 11, 2004. Some observers mark the date of his death as the end of the Second Intifada. Others regard the Intifada's end date as August 2005, occasioned by the completion of Israel's unilateral troop withdrawal from the Gaza Strip. Hamas claimed that Israeli withdrawal as its "victory." In any case, unresolved differences forced Palestinians and Israelis to look toward 2006 for the illusive solution to their problems.

Operation Defensive Shield

IDF soldiers in Nablus in 2002 during Operation Defensive Shield

Operation Defensive Shield was a large-scale military operation conducted by the IDF in the spring of 2002 during the Second Intifada. The operation came in response to the Hamas suicide bombing of the Passover Seder in Netanya. It was the largest military campaign in the West Bank since the Six-Day War of 1967, involving more than 20,000 IDF members.

"Operation Defensive Shield was first and foremost a question of decision making," said Colonel Amir Baram of the Israel Defense Forces. "We had to be victorious mainly over ourselves, overcome the fear and enter a densely populated area saturated with explosives and enemies. We learned more about ourselves from the decision than we did about the Palestinians."[6]

Beginning on March 29, IDF armor, infantry, and aircraft attacked the West Bank cities of Jenin, Bethlehem, Nablus, Qalqilya, and Ramallah. The fighting was up-close and personal. "We had no qualms at all about the activity," Baram added. "We were defending our home. It wasn't hard to persuade soldiers that they were arresting suicide bombers who otherwise would kill their families in the center of the country."[7]

Israeli troops withdrew in early May. In 2003, Hamas suicide bombings dropped off about 50 percent from the previous year.

Supporters of former ruling party Fatah stand above the marquee and atop the roof of the Palestinian Legislative Council building in Ramallah, West Bank, on January 28, 2006. From their perilous perches on the Palestinian parliament, the gunmen fired shots in the air and demanded the resignation of the Fatah leadership.

CHAPTER 5
A Way Forward

In January, 2006, Hamas ran as a political party in elections for the Palestinian Legislative Council. It won a surprise victory over Fatah, taking 74 seats in the 132-seat parliament while Fatah had just 45. The United States, the European Union (EU), and other countries boycotted the new Hamas government. This created financial and humanitarian hardship in the Palestinian territories. Hamas also encountered strained relations with both Palestinian Authority President Mahmoud Abbas of the Fatah party and the PLO.

President George W. Bush, exercising his usual firm support for Israel, declared, "The United States does not support a political party that wants to destroy our ally Israel . . . it means you're not a partner in peace and we are interested in peace."[1] The rivalry between Hamas and Fatah continued. They would eventually form a coalition, but not before engaging in several violent exchanges.

In June, Hamas and other militants executed a tunnel raid near the Kerem Shalom military base on Israel's side of the Gaza border. The raiders killed two Israeli soldiers and kidnapped Corporal Gilad Shalit. Israel arrested Hamas legislators and leaders.

The following month, Hezbollah launched an attack on Israel from southern Lebanon. Firing nearly 4,000 Katyusha rockets into Israel, it killed eight Israeli soldiers and abducted two others. Israel responded with artillery fire, air strikes, and a ground invasion. The incursion ended with a cease-fire on August 14, after

claiming the lives of 121 Israeli soldiers and 44 civilians. Lebanese dead totaled more than a thousand, mostly civilians.

Hamas remained defiant. “This war has had a huge negative effect on the Israeli street,” said a Hamas negotiator, “and it has sent a message that the occupation can never stand against the resistance if you have a really good resistance.”[2]

In September 2006, fighting erupted between Hamas and Fatah and continued through December, leaving many dead. The fighting carried over into 2007, paralyzing the streets of Gaza.

Finally, on February 8, the two rivals signed the Mecca Agreement. The agreement called for power-sharing and the formation of a National Unity Government. “The Mecca agreement has laid the foundation for a power-sharing process that will

Passersby in the background view a burned-out vehicle, still aflame and smoking. The wreckage gives evidence of a clash between security officers and a newly created paramilitary force deployed on May 22, 2006 by the Hamas-led government in Gaza City. Heavy fighting erupted between the rival Hamas and Fatah factions. The driver of Jordan’s ambassador died in the violence that wounded at least seven Palestinians.

Arab leaders meet in the Islamic holy city of Mecca, Saudi Arabia, on February 8, 2007. Saudi Arabia's King Abdullah (center) applauds, along with Palestinian President Mahmoud Abbas (third from left), Hamas leader Khaled Meshaal (third from right), and other Arab officials, after agreeing to end the fighting in Gaza. The agreement followed weeks of factional violence and a yearlong international embargo against the Hamas government. It omitted any reference to a formal recognition of the state of Israel.

produce a functioning government capable of attending to our people's needs," noted Hamas's Khaled Meshaal. "It will also pave the way for rebuilding the PLO to include all the factions and become the legitimate representative of all Palestinian people."[3]

In March, a new government was sworn in, but violence broke out again in Gaza in June. Abbas dissolved the Hamas-led government and declared a state of emergency. Hamas remained in control of the Gaza Strip, while a Fatah-led emergency cabinet took control of the West Bank. Hamas and Israel continued to attack each other across the Gaza border.

After another year of hostilities, Hamas and Israel entered into a mutual six-month cease-fire agreement on June 18, 2008. During the summer, hostile exchanges kept Hamas and Fatah at odds with each other.

When the Hamas-Israeli truce agreement ended on December 19, Hamas declined to renew it. Instead, on Christmas Eve, Palestinian militants in Gaza pumped more than 60 rockets into Israel. Three days later, Israel responded with a series of air strikes targeting Hamas. They were the strongest in years. After a week of air strikes, Israel launched a ground invasion. It lasted for three weeks, claiming more than a thousand lives and leaving tens of thousands homeless. Hamas and Israel both declared a cease-fire on January 18, 2009.

In more recent times, long periods of **détente** became the norm. The Israeli government described these periods of mutual restraint as "quiet for quiet." But occasional Hamas rocket fire, followed by Israeli air strikes known as "mowing the lawn,"[4] periodically interrupted the "quiet."

In March 2012, Egypt brokered a cease-fire that ended another round of fighting. Israel successfully called for Hamas to police the withholding of rocket fire and the restraining of radical groups in Gaza. As an indication of Hamas's effectiveness in its enforcement role, 63 rockets were fired into Israel from Gaza in 2013, compared to 2,327 the previous year. But any goodwill emanating from the reduced rocket fire soon ran out. In April 2014, Israel broke off peace talks with the Palestinians. The Israelis indicated that a planned reconciliation between moderate Palestinians and Hamas militants would render any future negotiation impossible.

On July 8, 2014, in response to a new round of Hamas rocket fire, Israel launched Operation Protective Edge, and invaded the

An Israeli artillery battery and its stockpile of ordnance near Israel's border with the Gaza Strip on July 25, 2014, during Operation Protective Edge.

Gaza Strip again. The initial Israeli objective of stopping the rocket fire later expanded to include the destruction of the Gaza tunnel system. As many as 2,189 Gazans and 540 Israelis died in the conflict, before the Israelis withdrew on August 5. An open-ended cease-fire was declared three weeks later.

Israeli-Palestinian peace talks have remained on hold from 2014 to the present. Hamas operates pretty much underground in the West Bank. Its social and military infrastructure has been dismantled, and many of its members arrested by PA and Israeli security forces. Many Palestinians view Fatah's cooperation with the security services as an obvious attempt to undermine its long-standing rivalry with Hamas.

Over the years, numerous solutions to the problem have been proposed. Three stand out: the two-state solution, the destruction

Palestinian police officers loyal to Hamas stand at attention before a Palestinian flag and a patriotic banner during a graduation ceremony in Gaza City on March 30, 2017.

of one side, and the one-state solution. Most peacemakers champion the two-state solution, but it has proved to be ridden with thorny details and so far unacceptable to one side or the other.

In the destruction of one side, an Israeli victory would turn the Palestinians into second-class citizens in an **apartheid**-like society or possibly cause their expulsion from their homeland. On the other hand, a Palestinian conquest would subjugate Israelis and lead to a resumption of the conflict. Both results are unacceptable on their face.

Though a one-state solution worked in South Africa, it would likely not work between the Palestinians and Israelis. The Arab population growth would soon reduce the Israelis to a minority status and recreate the Arab-Israeli stand-off in reverse. This would also be unacceptable to both parties.

People of good faith on both sides must look for a fresh and innovative solution to a complex problem with a conciliatory spirit if a way forward is ever to be found. Today, the Israeli-Palestinian question remains unresolved and begs an answer.

Continuing Conflict

Palestinian President Mahmoud Abbas referred to a series of attacks against Israelis from September 2015 to early 2017 as part of a peaceful uprising; Israelis called it a wave of terror. Hamas- and Fatah-inspired militants were unrelenting in their search for new and innovative ways to spread terror.

According to figures released by the Israeli Ministry of Foreign Affairs in January 2017, terrorist attacks killed 46 people and injured another 649 (including four Palestinians) during this time span. Those attacks were varied—169 stabbings, 104 attempted stabbings, 128 shootings, 54 vehicular attacks, and one vehicle (bus) bombing.

Hamas, in its year-end report for 2016, claimed that it killed 17 Israelis and wounded another 437 during the year. In December, Hamas leader Khaled Meshaal said in Istanbul that his group "is smuggling weapons and digging tunnels in Gaza to prepare for a confrontation with [Israel] which will taste its woes on the edge of the Gaza Strip."[5] Meanwhile, Israel is constructing a $530-million underground barrier to prevent Hamas tunnels from accessing Israel territory. Point, counterpoint, and the beat goes on.

In December 2016, the UN Security Council passed a resolution demanding a halt to Israeli settlement building in Palestinian territory. Israeli Prime Minister Benjamin Netanyahu vowed not to comply with the resolution. In retaliation, he suspended ties with 12 countries that voted for it. On January 22, 2017, Israel announced plans to build almost 600 new settlement homes in occupied East Jerusalem, a move not likely to advance the peace process.

Currently, Israeli-Palestinian peace talks remain on hold. Hamas is admittedly preparing for further confrontation with Israel, while Israel continues to move ahead with its settlement building. Chances of an early solution to the Israeli-Palestinian issue appear unlikely at best.

TIMELINE

1516 Palestine comes under the rule of the Ottoman Empire.

1914 World War I begins; it ends in 1918.

1917 British government issues the Balfour Declaration on November 2.

1920 Victorious Allies divide up the Ottoman Empire at San Remo, Italy.

1921 Sheikh Izz ad-Din al-Qassam arrives in Haifa.

1922 League of Nations limits the boundary of Palestine and calls Transjordan a separate mandate; both rulings take effect in 1923.

1928 Hassan al-Banna founds the Muslim Brotherhood in Egypt.

1929 Arabs riot in Hebron.

1930 Qassam founds the Black Hand militant group.

1935 British police kill Qassam in a shootout near Jenin on November 19.

1936 Great Arab Revolt in Palestine begins; it ends in 1939.

1946 Muslim Brotherhood opens its first branch in Palestine.

1947 United Nations votes in November to establish two states in Palestine, one for Jews and one for Arabs.

1948 Jews proclaim the independent state of Israel on May 14, touching off the Arab-Israeli War of 1948.

1956 Arabs and Israelis fight a war over the Suez Canal.

1964 Palestine Liberation Organization (PLO) is founded in May.

1967 Arabs and Israelis clash in the Six-Day War; Israel occupies captured territories.

1973 Arabs and Israelis clash again in the Yom Kippur War.

1978 Egypt and Israel sign the Camp David Accords.

1982 Israel invades Lebanon; withdraws in 1985.

1983 Ahmad Yassin starts preparing for jihad by urging his followers to collect firearms.

1986 Yassin authorizes the creation of a security apparatus.

1987 First Intifada (uprising) begins; it ends in 1993.

1988 Hamas publishes its charter in August.

1989 Hamas carries out its first attack against Israel.

1991 Hamas forms the Izz ad-Din al-Qassam Brigades. Madrid Conference convenes.

1992 Israel deports more than 400 Hamas and Islamic Jihad activists to Lebanon.

1993 Israel and the PLO sign the Oslo Accords in Norway.

1998 Israel and the Palestinian Authority sign the Wye Memorandum.

2000 Israelis and Palestinians fail to reach a peace agreement at Camp David. Israeli opposition leader Ariel Sharon tours the Temple Mount, igniting the Second Intifada which ends in 2005.

2001 Ariel Sharon is elected as Israel's prime minister.

2002 Hamas suicide bomber bombs Passover Seder in the Park Hotel in Netanya. Israel launches Operation Defensive Shield in March; it ends in May.

2004 Israeli airstrike kills Ahmad Yassin. Yasser Arafat dies on November 11; Mahmoud Abbas replaces him as chairman of the PLO.

2006 Hamas runs as a political party and wins a majority in the Palestinian parliament. Hezbollah fires nearly 4,000 rockets into Israel. Fighting erupts between Hamas and Fatah and carries over into 2007.

2007 Hamas and Fatah sign the Mecca Agreement.

2008 Hamas and Israel enter into a six-month cease-fire agreement. Fighting breaks out again on Christmas Eve.

2009 Hamas and Israel declare another cease-fire in January.

2012 Egypt brokers another cease-fire to end another round of fighting between Israel and Hamas. Mohamed Morsi becomes first democratically elected Egyptian president.

2014 Abdel Fattah el-Sisi replaces the deposed Mohammed Morsi as Egyptian president. Israel launches Operation Protective Edge in July to end Hamas rocket attacks; it ends in August. Hamas introduces vehicular homicide attacks on Israeli citizens.

2015 Palestinian terrorist stabs and seriously wounds an Israeli policeman in the Old City of Jerusalem.

2016 United States approves $38 billion for military aid to Israel over the next 10 years.

2017 Palestinian truck driver deliberately drives his vehicle into a group of Israeli soldiers, killing four and injuring more than a dozen others.

CHAPTER NOTES

Chapter 1 Bitter Root

1. Ben Hartman, "Massacre survivors mark 10-years at Netanya Hotel." *The Jerusalem Post*, March 28, 2012. http://www.jpost.com/landedpages/printarticle.aspx?id=263711
2. Ibid.
3. Joel Leyden, "Israel Remembers the Passover Massacre." Israel News Agency. April 14, 2014. http://joelleyden.blogspot.com/2014/04/israel-remembers-passover-massacre.html
4. Ibid.
5. Ibid.
6. Beverley Milton-Edwards and Stephen Farrell, *Hamas: The Islamic Resistance Movement* (Malden, MA: Polity Press, 2010), p. 22.

Chapter 2 Partition and Protest

1. Azzam Tamimi, *Hamas: A History from Within* (Northampton, MA: Olive Branch Press, 2011), p. 3.
2. Beverley Milton-Edwards and Stephen Farrell, *Hamas: The Islamic Resistance Movement* (Malden, MA: Polity Press, 2010), p. 19.
3. Tamimi, *Hamas*, p. 52.
4. Avraham Sela, ed., *The Continuum Political Encyclopedia of the Middle East*. Revised and Updated Ed. (New York: Continuum, 2002), p. 691.

Chapter 3 First Intifada

1. Matthew Levitt, *Hamas: Politics, Charity, and Terrorism in the Service of Jihad* (New Haven: Yale University Press, 2006), p. 31.
2. U.S. Department of State, Office of the Historian, "The Madrid Conference, 1991." https://history.state.gov/milestones/1989-1992/madrid-conference
3. Beverley Milton-Edwards and Stephen Farrell, *Hamas: The Islamic Resistance Movement* (Malden, MA: Polity Press, 2010), p. 150.

Chapter 4 Second Intifada

1. Amnesty International. "Israel and the Occupied Territories: Broken Lives–A Year of Intifada." http://www.amnesty.org/en/library/info/MDE15/083/2001/en

2. Beverley Milton-Edwards and Stephen Farrell, *Hamas: The Islamic Resistance Movement* (Malden, MA: Polity Press, 2010), p. 100.

3. Ibid.

4. Ibid., p. 107.

5. Ibid., p. 110.

6. Avi Issacharoff and Amos Harel, "Recollections of Israel's Operation Defensive Shield, ten years later." *Haaretz*. March 30, 2012. http://www.haaretz.com/weekend/week-s-end/recollections-of-israel-s-operation-defensive-shield-ten-years-later-1.421639

7. Ibid.

Chapter 5 A Way Forward

1. Beverley Milton-Edwards and Stephen Farrell, *Hamas: The Islamic Resistance Movement* (Malden, MA: Polity Press, 2010), p. 262.

2. Ibid., p. 274

3. Azzam Tamimi, *Hamas: A History from Within* (Northampton, MA: Olive Branch Press, 2011), p. 246.

4. Zachary Laub, "Hamas." Council on Foreign Relations. August 1, 2014. http://www.cfr.org/israel/hamas/p8968

5. "Hamas Boasts That It Killed 17 Israelis in 2016." Bridges for Peace, January 4, 2017. https://www.bridgesforpeace.com/2017/01/hamas-boasts-killed-17-israelis-2016/

PHOTO CREDITS: Cover design elements: Bram Janssens/Dreamstime.com, StanOd/iStock/Getty Images Plus, Natis76/Dreamstime.com, and Sharon Beck; Interior design elements—Jupiterimages/liquidlibrary/Getty Images Plus, malija/iStock/Getty Images Plus, macrovector/iStock/Getty Images Plus, prudkov/iStock/Getty Images Plus, estherpoon/iStock/Getty Images Plus, and Sharon Beck. Photos: Cover, p. 1—Getty Images/Stringer/Getty Images News; p. 3—Yorrico/Dreamstime.com; p. 5—Congressional Research Service (CRS)/Public domain; p. 5 (globe)—Harvepino/iStock/Getty Images Plus; pp. 6, 13—Cam99/Stringer/Getty Images News; pp. 9, 10—Scott Nelson/Stringer/Getty Images News; p. 12—Rafy/cc by-sa 3.0; p. 14—ALFRED/SIPA/1111291834 (Sipa via AP Images); p. 17—Associated Press; p. 19—Getty Images/Handout/Getty Images News; p. 20—AP PHOTO/Brian Hendler/Associated Press; p. 24—Abid Katib/Stringer/Getty Images News; p. 25—Daniel Berehulak/Staff/Getty Images News; p. 27—Courtney Kealy/Stringer/Getty Images News; p. 30—REUTERS/Alamy Stock Photo; p. 31—Standing Guard in Nablus/Israel Defense Forces/cc by-sa 2.0; p. 32—Zahran Hammad/Stringer/Getty Images News; p. 34—Abid Katib/Staff/Getty Images News; p. 35—Suhaib Salem-Pool/Pool /Pool /Getty Images News; p. 37—Ilia Yefimovich/Stringer/Getty Images News; p. 38—Ashraf Amra/APA Images/ZUMA Wire/Alamy Live News.

PRINCIPAL PEOPLE

Mahmoud Abbas (MAHK-mood ab-BAS)—President of the State of Palestine and Palestinian National Authority.

Yasser Arafat (YAS-suhr ar-uh-FAT—Former leader of the Palestinian Liberation Organization (PLO) and the Palestine Authority (PA).

Hassan al-Banna (hah-SAHN al-ban-NUH)—Egyptian political and religious leader who founded the Muslim Brotherhood in 1928.

Ehud Barak (eh-HOOD buh-RAHK)—Prime minister of Israel from 1999 to 2001.

George H. W. Bush—Forty-first President of the United States.

Bill Clinton—Forty-second President of the United States.

Mikhail Gorbachev (mik-HILE GAWR-buh-chawf)—President of the Soviet Union from 1985 to 1991.

Theodor Herzl (THEO-dor HERT-sehl)—Hungarian Jew and Zionist founder.

Khaled Meshaal (KHAY-lihd meh-SHAHL)—Palestinian political leader and leader of Hamas since 2004.

Mohamed Morsi (mo-HAHM-ed MORE-see)—First democratically elected president of Egypt; served from 2012 to 2013.

Benjamin Netanyahu (BEN-juh-min neh-tahn-YAH-hoo)—Prime minister of Israel from 1996 to 1999 and from 2009 to present.

Abdel Basset Odeh (AHB-dehl BAH-seht OH-duh)—Hamas suicide bomber who self-destructed at the Park Hotel in Netanya, Israel, at the Passover Seder in 2002.

Izz ad-Din al-Qassam (iz ad-DEEN al-kahs-SAHM)—Syrian-born Palestinian Muslim preacher who was a leader in the fight against British, French, and Zionist organizations in the Middle East in the 1920s and 1930s; founder of the Black Hand militant group.

Yitzhak Rabin (YIHTS-hahk rah-BEEN)—Prime minister of Israel from 1974 to 1977 and from 1992 until his assassination in 1995.

Abbas al-Sayyad (ah-BAHS al-sai-EED)—Hamas political leader in Tulkarm and covert head of the Qassam Brigades terrorist cell there.

Ariel Sharon (ah-ree-EHL shah-ROHN)—Prime minister of Israel from 2001 to 2006.

Salah Shehadeh (suh-LAH she-HAHD-eh)—Military leader of Hamas's Izz ad-Din al-Qassam Brigades.

Gazan Mohammed Yasji (guh-ZAHN mo-HAH-mehd YAHZ-jee)—Hamas activist.

Ahmad Yassin (ACH-mahd yaz-SEEN)—Founder and spiritual leader of Hamas.

GLOSSARY

acronym (AA-croh-nihm)—word formed from initial letters of several other words

apartheid (uh-PART-hite)—system of rigid segregation of two or more races, with one race exerting control over the other(s)

autonomy (ah-TAHN-uh-mee)—right or condition of self-government

coerce (coe-ERSS)—obtain something by using force or the threat of force

détente (day-TAUNT)—period of reduced tensions between rivals

Fatah (FAH-tah, or fah-TAH)—one of the largest militant political groups within the Palestine Liberation Organization (PLO)

Hamas (hah-MAHSS)—literally, "zeal" or "enthusiasm" in Arabic; also an acronym for *Harakat al-Muqawanna al-Islamiyya*, or Islamic Resistance Movement

Hezbollah (hehz-buh-LAH)—a radical Islamic group in Lebanon

infidel (IN-fuh-dehl)—person who doesn't believe in a particular religion

Islam (IS-lahm, or is-LAHM)—the Muslim religion, based on the teachings of Muhammad; the Muslim world

Islamic Jihad (ihz-LAH-mihk jih-HAHD)—a radical Palestinian group

League of Nations (LEEG of NAY-shuns)—organization for international cooperation and prevention of war formed after World War I

mandate (MAN-dayt)—authority to perform a certain task or apply certain policies

Mossad (moe-SAHD)—Israel's national intelligence service

overt (OH-vehrt)—done openly, not hidden

primeval (pry-MEE-vuhl)—the earliest ages in world history

profane (proh-FANE)—disrespectful of religious practice

secular (SEK-yew-lahr)—concerned with worldly affairs rather than spiritual ones; an opposition to or rejection of religion

Sharia law (shah-REE-uh LAW)—law based on the principles of Islam

waqf (waqf)—a religious endowment; property dedicated to religious use

Zionist (ZIE-uhn-ist)—referring to a movement founded in 1897 that sought and later achieved the founding and development of a Jewish homeland (now Israel) in Palestine

FURTHER READING

Burgan, Michael. *Terrorist Groups*. North Mankato, MN: Compass Point Books, 2010.

Downing, David. *The Debate about Terrorist Tactics*. Ethical Debates Series. New York: Rosen Publishing, 2008.

Landau, Elaine. *Suicide Bombers: Foot Soldiers of the Terrorist Movement*. Minneapolis, MN: Twenty-First Century Books, 2006.

Nardo, Don. *The History of Terrorism*. North Mankato, MN: Compass Point Books, 2010.

Netzley, Patricia D. *Terrorism and War of the 2000s*. San Diego, CA: ReferencePoint Press, 2014.

Sherrow, Victoria. *Homegrown Terror: The Oklahoma City Bombing*. Berkeley Heights, NJ: Enslow Publishers, 2013.

WORKS CONSULTED

Amnesty International. "Israel and the Occupied Territories: Broken Lives–A Year of Intifada." http://www.amnesty.org/en/library/info/MDE15/083/2001/en

Bridges for Peace. "Hamas Boasts That It Killed 17 Israelis in 2016." January 4, 2017. https://www.bridgesforpeace.com/2017/01/hamas-boasts-killed-17-israelis-2016/

Campo, Juan E., ed. *Encyclopedia of Islam*. New York: Checkmark Books, 2009.

Caridi, Paola. *Hamas: From Resistance to Government*. Trans. by Andrea Teti. New York: Seven Stories Press, 2012.

Gleis, Joshua L., and Benedetta Berti. *Hezbollah and Hamas: A Comparative Study*. Baltimore, MD: The Johns Hopkins University Press, 2012.

Hall, M. Clement, and the Charles River Editors. *The History of Hamas*. Cambridge, MA: Charles River Editors, 2014.

Harik, Judith Palmer. *Hezbollah: The Changing Face of Terrorism*. London, UK: I. B. Tauris, 2007.

Hartman, Ben. "Massacre survivors mark 10-years at Netanya Hotel." *The Jerusalem Post*, March 28, 2012. http://www.jpost.com/landedpages/printarticle.aspx?id=263711

Issacharoff, Avi, and Amos Harel. "Recollections of Israel's Operation Defensive Shield, ten years later." *Haaretz*. March 30, 2012. http://www.haaretz.com/weekend/week-s-end/recollections-of-israel-s-operation-defensive-shield-ten-years-later-1.421639

WORKS CONSULTED

Laub, Zachary. "Hamas." Council on Foreign Relations. August 1, 2014. http://www.cfr.org/israel/hamas/p8968

Levitt, Matthew. *Hamas: Politics, Charity, and Terrorism in the Service of Jihad*. New Haven, CT: Yale University Press, 2006.

Leyden, Joel. "Israel Remembers the Passover Massacre." Israel News Agency. April 14, 2014. http://joelleyden.blogspot.com/2014/04/israel-remembers-passover-massacre.html

Milton-Edwards, Beverley, and Stephen Farrell. *Hamas: The Islamic Resistance Movement*. Malden, MA: Polity Press, 2010.

Norton, Augustus Richard. *Hezbollah: A Short History*. Princeton, NJ: Princeton University Press, 2007.

Pargeter, Alison. *The Muslim Brotherhood: From Opposition to Power*. London, UK: Saqi Books, 2013.

Sekulow, Jay, with Jordan Sekulow, Robert W. Ash, and David French. *The Rise of ISIS: A Threat We Can't Ignore*. New York: Howard Books, 2014.

Sela, Avraham. *The Continuum Political Encyclopedia of the Middle East*. Revised and Updated Edition. New York: Continuum, 2002.

Tamimi, Azzam. *Hamas: A History from Within*. Northampton, MA: Olive Branch Press, 2011.

U.S. Department of State, Office of the Historian. "The Madrid Conference, 1991." https://history.state.gov/milestones/1989-1992/madrid-conference

ON THE INTERNET

Avishi, Bernard. "Mahmoud Abbas: Winning on Points." *The New Yorker*. June 4, 2014. http://www.newyorker.com/news/news-desk/mahmoud-abbas-winning-on-points

Whitaker, Brian. "UN report details West Bank wreckage." *The Guardian*. August 2, 2002. http://www.theguardian.com/world/2002/aug/02/israel

Witte, Griff, and William Booth. "As cease-fire with Hamas fails to take shape, Netanyahu says, 'Our answer is fire.'" *The Washington Post*. July 16, 2014. http://www.washingtonpost.com/world/israel-accepts-truce-plan-hamas-balks/2014/07/15/04373008-0bf5-11e4-8c9a-923ecc0c7d23_story.html

INDEX